AMONG MY TANGLED THOUGHTS

Alicia Hunter

When did the cost of living
become so expensive?
Working two full time jobs,
minimum wage
can't afford to eat.
The lampshade
needs to be dusted again,
as does the vase
that my grandmother bought.
She covers up
the bruises
with makeup in the mirror.
Will this be convincing enough
for them?
When will she realize
that she is better than this?
When will she realize her skin
was meant to be caressed?
Not bruised.
When will she put a stop
to his abuse?

His words do more damage
than her razor blades ever could.

I feel myself slowly disconnecting,
from everything,
again
and I don't know
if anything
can bring me back this time.

I've stopped counting
how many days I'm clean,
and started waking up
wishing,
I had taken
just a few more pills
the night before.
So that it was worse than stomach ache,
and easier
than dealing
with myself.

I felt the earth shake beneath me
open up to swallow me whole,
and I let her consume me.

My father,
was an addict.
He was addicted to drugs.
He was addicted to hurting others.
He was addicted to power.

My mother,
was an addict.
She was addicted to alcohol.
She was addicted to cigarettes.
She was holding things in.

That addictive trait,
has passed down to me.
I have the addiction;
to hold things in,
let them eat away at my soul.
I have the addiction
to self-destruct.
The addiction
to give too much of myself.

They are everywhere-
those sunflowers with the coal heart center.
They are so deceiving,
'So kind, so light', you think.
So you get close,
tell them everything.
That bright yellow so deceiving,
hiding their coal heart center.
They make you think
your best interest is at heart.
When you need them is when
they turn their back on you.
Exposing their coal heart center;
ripping out your heart
destroying anything beautiful
as though they think
that it would help with their ugly heart.
They destroy you
drag you down
D
  R
   O
    W
     N
      I
       N
        G
Until there is nothing left.

The early morning dew
sparkling in the rising sun
peaking over the horizon in the distance.
My bruised and cut hands wrap tighter
around the warm mug
containing what keeps me going day after day.
Dreadfully tired,
remembering dreams,
from the night before.
Not knowing what was imaginary,
and what was reality.
My mind is playing tricks on me again;
replaying the sound of the mirror,

S H A T T E R I N G

I glance at my chipped nail polish.
Know I need to fix it.
The coffee in this mug
is the only thing
keeping me from falling back
into nothingness.

Take my hand in yours
wipe away the pain
of false 'I love you's"
help me to forget all the sorrow
that has come before you.
Will you my darling,
be the one that can fix this broken soul?
can you take my hand in yours,
and make me matter again?

My god, I don't know anymore
nothing seems real-
I'm on the verge of a breakdown
and no one seems to notice.
I just feel like going
on a rage driven rampage.
I don't cry often,
but last night I cried my eyes dry.
My anxiety is bubbling over
and I feel like this is okay.
I'm contemplating suicide.
This is normal.
My god, I wish I was normal!
And my moms boyfriend
is convinced that we need
styrofoam plates instead.
I feel the breakdown,
I know it's coming.
I can feel it in my throat,
nagging at the back of my mind.
I wish it would all just go away!
my god, everywhere is filled
with negativity and yelling,

I can't escape.

I can't even get an hours worth of sleep,
and I can't show weakness,
for fear it bothers them.
I can't show sadness,
for fear it worries them.
My god, I just don't know anymore.

The way,
her hips sway
as she walks away,
has got me hypnotized.
The way her breath
tickles my ear
when she tells me she loves me
is driving me crazy.
The way she bites her lip
when I wrap my arms
around her waist
makes me wonder how
how I ever thought
I was in love
with anyone else.

Can this be real?

She doesn't realize
how easily she could destroy me.
Her hands are so gentle;
one wrong look from her
one perhaps a little less
filled with love
and I think
my heart
would shatter.

Outside my window,
there's a war.
A war between the sun,
and the storm.
Who will win?
clouds covering up

every

    last

        ray of light.

This is but a battle in a war
the sun
will shine again
and the storm will pass.
Inside my window-
inside of me,
there is a war.
A war between the sun,
and the storm…

No matter how hard I try
I can't seem
to strip him
from my mind.
It's as if he's fastened there,
like tawdry wallpaper.
And I can't seem
to scrub out the stains
he left on my heart,
like spilled red wine
on white carpet.
No matter how many showers I take,
I can't seem to wash him
off of me.
And I still hear his voice
when that song comes on.
I can't seem to wash him
out of my sheets.
And I still feel his strong arms
months after he's left.
I can't get rid of him
even though
he's already

Gone.

Someone asked me where,
where was home
and I almost said your name,
but I stopped myself
I realized they expected me
to say a place.
And I realized that you,
are gone.
And you are no longer
my home.
And no words can explain
how your eyes made me
stumble over my words.
How they could freeze the world
but you gave me frostbite instead.
And no words can explain
how your arms
made me feel safe,
made me feel like I was home.
And I swear you'll be the death of me,
because I'm burning myself alive
trying to forget the scars
you've left on my soul,
trying to melt the ice
you've left on my heart,
and I'm trying to forget you.
but you always find a way back into my head.
And soon I swear
I'll be nothing more
than a smoldering pile
of self-destruction.

And someone asked me,
where was home.
And I almost said your name
but I choked on my words
as they were about to slip out of my mouth.
And someone asked me
where was home,
and All I could think about
was you…
And now all I try to do,
is fall asleep
before I fall apart.
Because I can't stop thinking of you.

It's the morning after
and I'm hungover
on her touch
on the sweet nothings
she whispered in my ear
as she pressed her smooth palms
against my cheek
and traced the line of my jaw
slowly
reminding me of what
she could do,
what she is capable of.
What I don't trust her not to do.
and it's the reason why
I still flinch when she puts her arms around me.
I'm not hungover on the booze,
the shots,
the bottles of beer.
I'm hungover on her;
how she ran her hands slowly
down my back,
how she made me feel loved,
wanted,
desired.
It's the morning after
and I'm hungover on her
and everything about her.

I'm trying to sleep,
I'm overwhelmed
with a sense of
bittersweet nostalgia.
For you and our dalliance.
and I'm overflowing,
with a bittersweet nostalgia,
to once again be your
one and only cynouse
and for our short lived superstitious love.

And would you know
that everything
I've ever let go of
has claw marks
permanently embedded?
And nostalgia is a
spinner of lies
who tangles you in the delusion
that things were greater than they were.

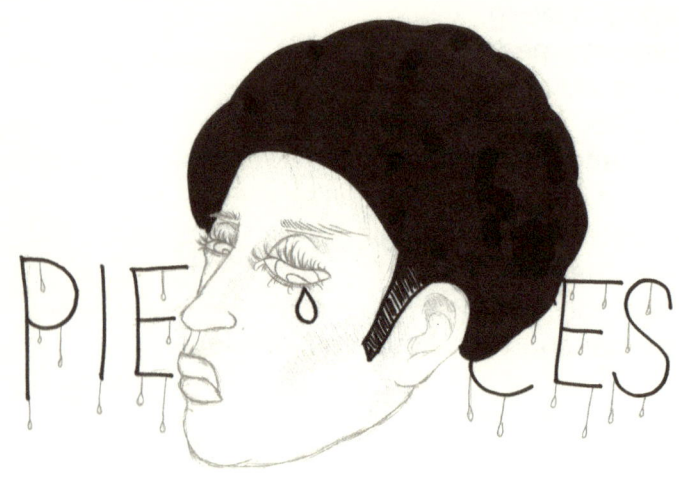

Lately I've been feeling like I don't belong.
Like the grounds I walk are not mine to walk on.
I swear I was doing okay.
I tried so hard to get better,
and I swear I was getting there.
I made so much progress.
I tried so hard to forget it all,
and move on.
And I thought I was getting to the point
where I could say
"Wow, I'm doing so much better!"
I was almost even happy.

I don't know what happened.
Something went wrong,
and now I find myself gasping for air.
And I don't know when it happened,
but I started losing my mind again.
I'm missing pieces of myself,
and I don't know how to find them.

Honestly, I hope
you *are* in love with her.
I hope she shows you what it feels like
to be happy,
to be wanted,
to be needed.
I hope you know how much
she loves you so.
I hope she gives you everything
you ever wanted
everything I couldn't give to you.
I hope she is the reason for you to smile
the reason you keep going.
And I hope that she
rips your heart out.
I hope she rips it out
and stomps it into the ground.
I hope she shows you what it's like
to have your very breath
stolen from your lungs.
I hope she takes everything she gave you
and walks away without a second thought.
I hope she leaves you,
like you left me.
So I hope that you are in love with her
and I hope that you are happy.
and Honestly,
I hope she rips your fucking heart out.

And I remember
how it felt
when you wrapped your cold hand
tightly around my wrist
pulled me closer
and stole that kiss.

And I remember
how it felt when
you wrapped your arm
around my waist in the elevator
and pressed your fingertips
into my hip.

And I remember
how it felt
when you ran your hand
up the inside of my thigh
underneath the meeting table.

And I remember
how it felt
when you smiled not only
with your mouth,
but with your eyes,
and how it made my soul melt.

And I remember
the way
my heart dropped
fell out of my chest
and onto the floor

when you said the things you said.

And I remember
how I felt
empty,
when you didn't show up
for nearly two weeks.

And I remember
the way
my stomach flipped
and my face lit up
when you finally came back
on a Tuesday.

And now
I don't know
what I feel,
or how I should feel.

And now all I know
is that the world I built around you
is crashing down around me.

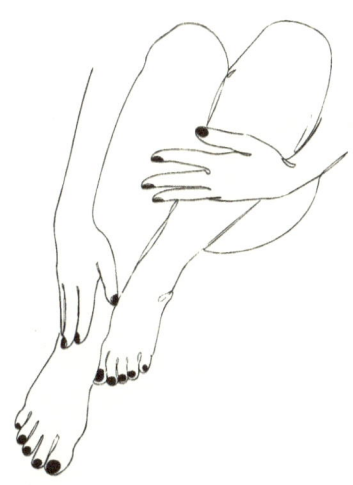

She had flaming orange hair,
and ice cold,
freezing eyes
I swear her eyes,
were almost as cold,
as her soul.

It's my own fault
I got hurt this time.
I shouldn't have let you in,
but when you held my heart
I felt so safe.
and it made me forget how much
this will hurt when it ends.

It's getting colder,
and so is my heart.
It's getting darker,
and so are my thoughts.
The leaves are falling,

Falling,

Falling.

And so am I.

Falling,

Falling,

Falling,

Falling apart...

I didn't ever mean
to love you like this.
I didn't ever mean,
for my heart to stop
for a few seconds
when you entered the room.
I didn't ever mean
for my eyes to get brighter,
and my face to turn red
at the mention of your name.
I didn't ever mean
for my stomach
to have bricks inside of it
every morning
you didn't show up.
And I didn't ever mean
for you to have this much control
over my state of mind.
I didn't ever mean,
to love you like this.

I pick my hands.
Trying not to freak out
when I hear fireworks
because the truth is
I'm afraid of the sound.
It reminds me of the way
I used to feel around you.
The way it felt like
we made fireworks together.
Even though those days are gone,
at times the past still scares me,
and I don't want to feel like I'm suffocating again.

THIS WEEK

I WAS TRYING TO DRINK HER FACE AWAY,

BUT I ONLY FORGOT WHAT DAY IT WAS

AND THE INTOXICATED THOUGHTS WERE HER.

IT'S ALWAYS HER

HER.

HER.

OH MY GODDESS, HER!

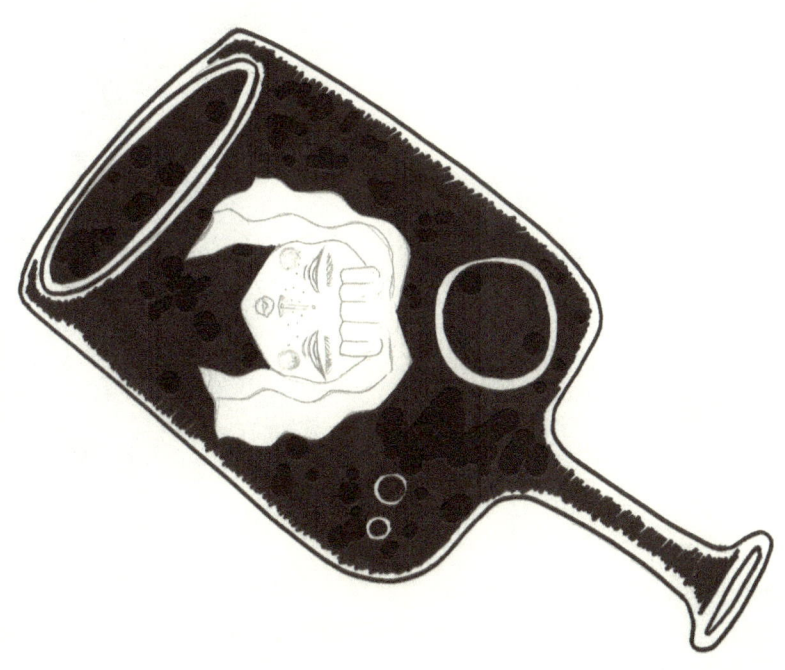

I'm sorry for always smelling like cigarette smoke,
and staring at you all the time.
I'm sorry for having so many scars,
and for hating myself all the time.
For talking about my problems, and probably,
being annoying as hell.
I'm sorry I can't go a day without crying,
I'm sorry I'm not good enough.
And for not being perfect
and having hands too shaky to hold
when you tell me beautiful words,
that were not meant for me.

And I'll spend my life lost,

among the moon and stars,

because they still remind me

of you…

I breathed him in like fresh raspberries,
and felt my lungs fill again.
I asked him his favorite flower,
he said there aren't enough petals for every time
I made him cry.
I write poems about flowers,
but can't manage to keep any alive.
I spent a whole summer not going to bed
until the sun was up because I thought the dark
was going to swallow me whole.
Consuming.
When I bleed,
I expect darkness to seep out.
My days are arranged by sadness;
I've cried at too many sunsets
and not enough sunrises.
I asked him where he felt the love and he said,
in his fingertips.
Maybe that's why it felt like cigarettes burning
every time he would touch me.
And still my skin feels as if it is on fire.
I won't be content with my body
until I can fit back in those shorts I wore last summer,
and I don't mind looking at it in a mirror.
Home still feels like just another empty word I don't fit
into.
I tasted pain when I kissed him,
and I've never broken a bone
but I guess that's my consolation prize
for a fragmented mind.
At twenty I'm still too small for most amusement rides,
but can fit in most swing sets.

These days I sleep with lavender stuffed inside my pillow
to try and keep the nightmares away.
I asked him if he believes in forever and he said,
he knows everything is temporary
but so do I.
My heart is reaching past my rib cage,
and I think one of these days it might vaporize
and evaporate right through the cracks.

Just the sound of his name
gives me chills.
It used to just make me weak
with sadness
and missing
and shame.
But now his name in my ears,
scares me.
It is a word I don't want to hear,
one I wish were permanently erased
from my memory.
It is two syllables that can destroy me,
within a few seconds.

Her hands were warm
and her heart was even warmer.
She was a fleece blanket
encircling you in those cold autumn months.
she was comforting,
and soft
and lovely.
The freezing storm raged on
long after you left her
and she has grown hot.
She is no longer warm
and comforting.
Her hands are no longer the soft warm touch
that they used to be.
Now
she is an inferno.
she is a flame refusing to be put out
and will burn anything
in her way.

She is no longer the soft warm girl
you used to know.
She is a blazing fire
that cannot be compared
to all of the stars in the sky.

When I looked into your eyes
I saw nothing except raw
and pure pain
and I knew then that you weren't capable of love,
let alone loving someone like me.
But the way you touched me...
Oh how your hands felt on my skin...
It was indescribable.
They didn't feel like electricity, like some people say.
And no, not like fire,
as I've felt before,
not gentle,
not rough.
your fingertips on my skin
felt like I imagine the ground does
when the sunlight falls upon it
after all of the harsh winter ice melts away.
And I haven't felt anything for so long,
when you touched me,
I felt something that I hadn't felt before.
And I won't say its love,
because I don't know what being in love is.
And I'm not sure if I even believe
in falling in love anymore.
You said you believed you could see
a person's intentions in their eyes.
Is that why you wouldn't look at me when you held
me?
Why, when you did, you made sure to look away
before I could find the lies hidding inside of them?

Why can't you see that my eyes aren't windows?
Can't you see that they're deep and dangerous wells
that boys so unlike you have fallen into
and never escaped?
They will lead you straight to absolutely nothing.
Because I've given my everything
to too many people who gave me
nothing.
And I gave what little I had left,
to you.
And you no longer have any use for me,
so I'm back to that feeling of... not feeling.
But darling,
I'd move the stars for you,
because I still believe you deserve nothing less than

Everything.

He asked me
"What makes you happy"
and all I could think of
was how happy I was
when I believed the lie,
that he loved me too…

All that I need to say to you
lies in those unsent messages.
All the questions unasked,
and unanswered.
Am I too much for you to handle?
Enough to make you leave?
Not enough for you to stay?
Do I even want to know?
Still the drafts pile up,
and I may never know.
The questions remain unanswered.

I'LL SPEND MY LIFE LOST IN THE SKY
BECAUSE IT STILL REMINDS ME OF YOU
AND I CAN'T HEAR YOUR VOICE
WHEN I LOOK AT THE STARS ANYMORE
I CAN'T REMEMBER THE LAST TIME YOU CALLED
BEFORE THE CRASH
BUT I CAN REMEMBER THE SOUND
OF YOUR TIRES SQUEAL
IN MY DREAM TWO NIGHTS BEFORE
AND I REMEMBER THE TIME
I FINALLY GOT THAT TELESCOPE
I'D WANTED FOR SO LONG
AND WE SPENT HOURS ON THE FRONT LAWN
WATCHING THE SKY
AND I REMEMBER ALL OF THOSE TIMES
WE SAT ON THE PORCH
WATCHING THE STORM CLOUDS ROLL IN
AND YOU TOLD ME TO COUNT THE SECONDS
BETWEEN THE FLASH OF LIGHTNING
AND THE CLAP OF THUNDER
TO TELL HOW FAR AWAY IT WAS
AND I CAN'T HELP BUT REMEMBER THESE
THINGS
AND I MISS YOU
I MISS YOU
EVEN THOUGH YOU WERE THE FIRST TO BREAK
ME
ALTHOUGH YOU SHOULD HAVE BEEN THE FIRST
TO LOVE ME

Fireworks were always your favorite.
the fourth was hard for me.
Every boom
shattered me even more.
Each clap
resonated inside of me,
Buried itself deep.
Every flash of beautiful color,
reminds me you are gone.
Forever this time.
And even after the chaos and beauty
of the fiery light show has passed,
my chest still aches.
There isn't a day that goes by
that I don't feel the rumbling in my chest,
pulling my pieces farther apart.
Will I be able
to string them back together this time?

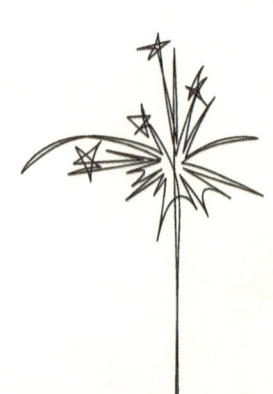

My heart has become
A mangled thing.
I'm not even sure
if It's mine anymore.
It has become calloused
and hard.
Cold to the things that once
made emotion pour out of me
like a flowing river of disaster:
Destroying everyone and everything in its path.
It seems everywhere i go,
disappointment follows,
but that's nothing new.
I've spent my whole life failing
to live up to what everyone thought I should be.
A disappointment.
Nothing more than wasted youth.
Nothing more than something to be disposed of.
And he said, "you're just like a cigarette.
Something someone puts in their mouth for a while,
and then stomps out on the ground."
And I can't help but think he was right,
when all I seem to be able to do
isn't good enough.
And I'm not really sure my heart
is a heart anymore.
Yet somehow she still manages to see the beauty in
it.
But my heart has grown calloused
and hard

And soon she will realize
I am not something worth bruising for.

How many days would it take
to count all the shells in the sea?
Or all the sand on the shore?
That's how long
it will take
to mend my broken heart
once you decide
I'm not enough,
or I'm too much.
It will take as many days
as it would to count
every damn drop of rain in the clouds
for me to become whole again,
once you decide to leave.

THEY SAY HOME IS WHERE THE HEART IS,

BUT YOU TOOK MY HEART AND LEFT ME HERE
WITHOUT ONE.

NOW I'M JUST A SHELL TRYING FIND SOMETHING
THAT MAKES

ME FEEL THE WAY YOU MADE ME FEEL.

AND I THINK I'LL BE THIS FOREVER.

AND I WILL ALWAYS REMEMBER YOU AS

MY FAVORITE ALMOST.

My doctor said
"You rely on your feelings as an identity"
and I won't say she's wrong,
because who am I if not what I feel?
If not what I feel,
then I am all the horrible things I've done.
I am every horrible thing
that has happened to me.
If I am not what I feel,
then I am cold and bitter
I am nothing more than everything I'm not.
My doctor says "Your feelings are fleeting,
constantly changing"
and so am I.
I am always changing-
always different.
Never the same as the moment before.
I am my mothers pouring from an
empty cup.
I am a bird with wings spread,
ready to take flight
At the first sign of trouble.
I am my fathers late night phone calls,
getting so high he can finally remember
who he's supposed to care about.
I am his lack of a suicide note.
I am my guilt for leaving,
my guilt for finally putting myself first.
I am how deeply I love,
how tightly I hold onto who I love,
I am the fight for them to stay,
I am the claw marks
permanently embedded
in everything I have ever let go of.
I am taking a whole bottle of antidepressants

because I feel they would be better off
without me here.
I am refusing to leave because I feel can
fix them,
save them.
I am fighting for what I believe in,
and I am afraid to stand up for myself.
My doctor says "you don't need to feel,
to know who you are."
But I do.
but through it all I am just
a shell in which the feelings reside
and I will shatter.

"Just take the pills," she says.

I WANTED TO BEG
"PLEASE DON'T GO"
BUT I COULD NOT MAKE MYSELF
BEG ONE MORE PERSON TO STAY
I COULD NOT LET MYSELF
SHOW YOU HOW MUCH I NEED YOU
BUT NOW I WISH I WOULD HAVE
BECAUSE MAYBE YOU'D BE HERE RIGHT NOW
NOW YOU'RE SOMEPLACE FAR FROM ME
NOW YOU'RE ON THE OTHER SIDE OF THE
COUNTRY
AND I'M SURE
YOU DIDN'T EVEN LOOK BACK
BEFORE YOU LEFT

IT'S 4AM
AND MY SHEETS ARE BLEEDING YOUR NAME
AND MY HEART IS SCREAMING FOR
REPENTANCE
AND THIS BOTTLE COULD NEVER
BE DEEP ENOUGH TO MAKE ME FORGET
ALL THE PAIN I'VE CAUSED US

And I'll never forget
how I shrunk myself for you.
How I broke myself down
into bite sized pieces
made for your mouth only.
And I'll never forget how all my thoughts are you you
you
even now when I'm broken,
and how I tried to be beautifully broken
but god dammit I'm just broken
and I'll never forget
how I watched the hate for me grow in your eyes
and how your touch grew colder and colder
and as your touch grew colder
I became more formable into what you wanted me to
be
and I'd be anything you wanted me to be.
I let you shape me- mold me
into what you wanted me to be
and I'll never forget the first time
I could see only my father in you,
and the same time I saw everything
that was wrong with you.
And how I stopped loving myself
ao I could only love you
because you had convinced me
that I wasn't worthy of you,
that somehow you were doing me a favor
by being with me
that you were saving me
but now I know the truth,

That the only thing saving me was me.
And here I am writing this goodbye,
knowing I'm stronger than I ever was.

She said "you feel like home"
and I can't help but think we're made from the same
stars
and now I'm drawing constellations in my freckles
and I've never felt more seen.
It's 2:22 am and I can't get you out of my head.
I write all my best poetry when I'm falling in love
or falling apart.
I can't tell which it is this time.

He made me feel
like I was worth something,
even when everything inside me
was screaming that I was nothing.
And when I wanted to tear open my skin
and crawl out of it
he made me feel like I was home.
And when I felt like a hostage
in my own body,
he made me feel safe.

I bought a poetry book
titled Nineteen
but now I'm twenty
and I still haven't read it.
I think it's poetic-
symbolic even
how my mind has let the time slip by
years blend together
and memories dissolve into nothingness.

It seems with every passing year,
every new trauma
the fog gets thicker...

Tightening...

Tightening...

Tightening...

withholding-

What happened to me?

I've tried writing of this for months,
triggering myself for the sake of a good piece.
but the truth is
there's nothing poetic about it.
Nothing poetic about being afraid
nothing poetic about trying
to drink myself to death
and passing out on the sidewalk
outside of the bar.
Nothing poetic about packing my bags
and running away.
Nothing poetic about
most days being more victim
than survivor.
Nothing poetic about
wishing to cut myself out of my skin
to finally feel at home in my body again.
Nothing poetic about
being the 98%

When I was 18.
When I was 15.
When I was 13.
And when I was 7.

I am the 98%.

The worst part about healing
is the inability to
fully engulf myself in every emotion.
I can't pick at my scars
like scabs on scraped knees
spilling the darkest parts of myself
onto the page
anymore.
And I'm not too skilled at writing of the worlds beauty
when all I've lived is its dark underbelly.

Everywhere I go in this town is laced with trauma.
'Round every corner is a trigger.
This place is nothing but wasted potential
and missed opportunities.
I am a shell of what I could have been.
First born and first forgotten.
I've been spiraling
and it doesn't look like poetry
as broken things often do.
The laundry has been piling up again
And so have the boxes.
I think I might hold onto them
in case I decide to pick up and leave this place

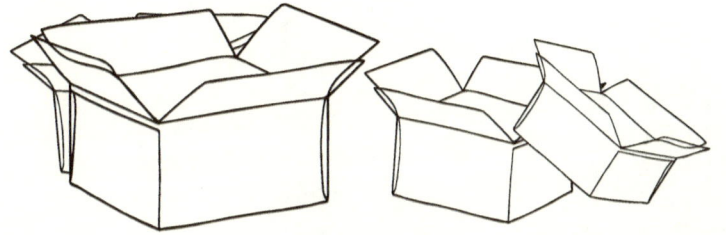

Healing, as I've heard,
is not linear.
And on days like this it seems
I am ever reaching for some
unattainable goal of wholeness.
The truth is
I'll always be missing pieces.

I am filled with an unbearable dread
and I need someone to pluck it out
like a poison thorn
you stuck into me,

l e e c h i n g .

I swear I'll never forget
how you grabbed my hand
and screamed "run"
as we dashed out of the theater
into the cold December air.
I'm still dreaming of you,
waking up smelling cigarettes and
strawberry stems still pressed
between pages
of poems we wrote
inspiring each other till daylight,
drunk on each other's words.
Gemini moon,
the intimacy of a best friend
turned lover.

My mother showed me how
to never let a man consume you.
I will always have an out-
a way to leave.
I decided young never to marry.

My mother showed me how
you can leave the ones you love most,
and I am my mothers daughter.
So I will sharpen my teeth
so my words are like daggers
and I will line my lips
with the blood of those
whom could not respect me.

Loving her
is looking into a mirror
and learning to love myself.

I pass patches of crimson red clovers
on my way to work
every day and I think of you.
I'm scared that when they wither away,
our love may too.

Summer love of
flowers pressed between the pages,
she's showing me how to love again.
I'm learning that love
can truly be soft
and patient
and kind.

When she touches me
it brings tears to my eyes
I've never been loved so tenderly.
it's cathartic
tracing I love yous into my skin.

Sometimes my throat closes up
and I can't tell if it's anxiety
or an allergic reaction.
So I'll lie down and pretend
it's neither.
Is it my body that betrayed me
or my mind this time?
Neither have ever seemed
to be on my side.

Growing up
a child too young to understand
the grip of addiction.
A childhood wound passed down
festering in each generation.

TOMB.

I wish I could remember you
laughing on the front porch,
the tap tap tap
before you open a new pack of cigarettes.
Talking of newly discovered music.
But dreams of creating
were stolen from you.
You passed down to me
the suffocating expectations,
living under the thumb
of those who came before you.
You were the first to clip my wings,
to leave bruises on my soul.

I'm not so sure
I should let anyone love me
I am a heavy load to bear.
I am a ponderous burden
and I will pull you down
into pools of my own blood,
my insides are leaking out.

I love you is a curse
coming from my lips.
Dooming the receiver to an agony
where peace should be.

I am finding myself again
in the flicker of a fire
in the dark of night.
in the honey stirred into teas
and flower filled baths.
In the pages of old books
and the burning of cedar.
In the sparkle of starlight
and the moon's soft glow.

Discovering and loving
each new version of myself.

About The Author

Born a virgo of the first millennium, I was grown before I grew up. Growing up a child of a single mother turned me into a strong, independent, activist that goes after what she wants. Through every trauma and trial my mother has always been my rock. There's no way I would be shaped into the woman I am today without her support. I will forever admire the sacrifices she made to get me here and the wisdom she accumulated on the way.

These poems will forever tell you more than I could here. It's been a lifelong dream of mine to become a published author. Even through all the push back from people who were supposed to support me I feel as though it's written in the stars for my work to be out there! I've always been told to be realistic about my life goals and now I've made my dreams come true.

If you've reached the end of this book I encourage you to find healing within these pages or within your own. Dive deep into what made you and stare it right in the face.

Acknowledgements

Merona
Illustrations (15,20,29,59,67)

Sarah Simpson
Editing & Encouragement

Andrew Ramsey
Formatting & Cover